AF647424

Concept Publishing Co.
Rs. 125/--

DECENTRALISED PLANNING AND PANCHAYATI RAJ

Decentralised Planning and Panchayati Raj

(Proceedings of the D T Lakdawala Memorial Symposium)

MALCOLM S. ADISESHIAH
PRANAB MUKHERJEE
RAMAKRISHNA HEGDE
ASHIM DASGUPTA
GEORGE FERNANDES

INSTITUTE OF SOCIAL SCIENCES, NEW DELHI

&

CONCEPT PUBLISHING COMPANY, NEW DELHI

The Institute of Social Sciences has an ongoing research programme on Panchayati Raj in India. At present the Institute is carrying out a nation-wide study to generate data and evolve a critical understanding on the present status and future prospects of local governance in various states. Enhancing public awareness about the crucial role of Panchayati Raj in grassroots level democracy, decentralised planning and development is another objective. This publication forms part of this study.

Support for the study has come from the Ford Foundation.

All rights reserved. No part of this work may be reproduced, stored in a retrieval system, or transmitted in any form or by any means, electronic, mechanical, photocopying, recording or otherwise, without the prior written permission of the copyright owners and the Publishers.

ISBN 81-7022-496-9

First Published 1994

© Institute of Social Sciences, New Delhi

Published by
Ashok Kumar Mittal
Concept Publishing Company
A/15-16 Commercial Block
Mohan Garden
New Delhi 110 059

Layout by
Institute of Social Sciences
B-7/18 Safdarjung Enclave
New Delhi 110 029

Photograph

D T Lakdawala

D. T. Lakdawala

(1916 – 1992)

BORN in 1916 in Surat, Dhanshukhlal Tulsidas Lakdawala, affectionately called 'Saheb' was a product of the then school of Economics and Sociology, University of Bombay. He started his career as a faculty member in the same Department in the early 1940s and subsequently rose to become its Director – a position he held till 1978 – the year he retired from the University.

Dr. Lakdawala's specialisation was public finance and fiscal policy. His early work including his PhD dissertation was on justice in taxation. The concept of justice was important to him throughout his life. This was reflected in his special concern for the interests of the vast millions of unorganized workers of the country, who in Lakdawala's view, had been continuously neglected in the face of aggressive demands by the organized work force.

Dr. Lakdawala had endeared himself to the working class in this country through the two consumer price index committees he headed. The first was in 1958 to examine whether the expenditure pattern of the working class in Bombay city had undergone change since 1932-33; the second was in 1963 to examine the readjustment in the then existing series of consumer price index numbers, more particularly with respect to the housing index and its linking up with the new series.

Lakdawala Committee found the practice of freezing the housing index objectionable. It was corrected and linked to the 1960-based series. Consequently, thanks to Lakdawala, the industrial workers were saved the loss that they would have otherwise suffered in the transition from the old to the new index.

The five pillars of Lakdawala's economics were: a high rate of growth of agricultural commodities, the public provision for minimal collective needs, a low inflation rate, a substantial moderation in the satisfaction of the organized workers' demands and progressive taxation. His wide areas of interest in teaching and research included industrial and labour economics, economics of education, public policy and planning.

As the Deputy Chairman of the Planning Commission (1977-80), Dr. Lakdawala's major contribution was to conditionalize the growth rate with the proviso of reduction in the proportion of people below the poverty line. Besides, he also advocated a higher calorie norm for the rural poor.

In Prof. Lakdawala we had an advocate for decentralised planning. At the Institute of Social Sciences, Dr. Lakdawala encouraged and helped chart research studies in political and economic decentralization. Lakdawala had contributed a chapter "Decentralisation of Economic Power", in one of the earliest publications of the Institute: *Panchayati Raj in Karnataka Today: Its National*

Dimensions, in which he had written: "The logic of decentralization is so powerful that it has been almost universally accepted. It is now a well recognised doctrine that since local resources are to be harnessed, local needs to be consulted, and local knowledge is needed, a large degree of decentralization is essential for the success of developmental efforts. This is especially so for those developmental efforts which aim at transforming the lives of the people or where the masses are involved" Then he went on to say, "It is no use transferring functions and powers unless we also transfer the wherewithals with which to discharge the functions".

Dr. Lakdawala was a recipient of several awards including the prestigious Dadabhai Nauroji Award twice, for his pioneering work in economics. His wide ranging interest in economic problems coupled with his ability to examine them in a balanced way and work out practical solutions made Lakdawala an ideal chairman/member of several committees at the national and state levels.

Apart from hard core economics, another facet of Dr. Lakdawala's work was the area of institutional building. He was the founder-director of the Sardar Patel Institute of Economic and Social Research, Ahmedabad, and was also the honorary director of the Bombay based Centre for Monitoring Indian Economy. He remained involved full time with both these institutions until his sudden death. He also served as the Chairman of the Governing Boards of a number of social science research institutions in the country including the Institute of Social Sciences, New Delhi. The Institute is indebted to him for his guidance and support since its very inception.

"In Lakdawala's death", to quote Prof. P. R. Brahmananda, his student, colleague and long time associate, "the vast masses of the poor have lost a dependable friend; the students have lost a teacher who moulded them by example; the fraternity of economists has lost one who combined sharp analytical rigour with experienced wisdom; and the world is poorer by a good and honest man, whom power could not corrupt, wealth could not buy and misfortune could not embitter".

In memory of, and as a humble tribute to, this eminent economist who above all was extraordinarily humane, the Institute of Social Sciences organised a symposium on "Decentralised Planning" on September 24, 1992 at the India International Centre Auditorium, New Delhi.

CONTENTS

PREFACE

ALL of us, who knew Prof. Lakdawala either personally or through his work, remember him today for his contribution to economics and broadly to the area of social sciences as well as to the Indian society at large. His untimely death has removed from us a doyen among social scientists.

I had the privilege of working with Prof. Lakdawala in the last years of his life and I learnt immensely from the great scholar that he was. Right from the Institute of Social Sciences' inception in 1985, Prof. Lakdawala was keen that such an institute should systematically study and research into contemporary social and political problems using an interdisciplinary framework. And further, he strongly desired that the findings of such studies should not remain confined to certain intellectual circles, but be made available to the members of decision-making organizations, government bodies, trade unions, people's organizations and scientific communities, so as to enlarge their options for action. He used to periodically review the progress we were making in this direction. My last meeting with him was in Bombay just a fortnight before his untimely death.

Well-known economists in the country have written about Prof. Lakdawala's contribution to economics. I would like to highlight just two aspects. First, his contribution to the construction of the consumer price index which affected the working class. It is well-known how the Lakdawala Committee examined the expenditure pattern of the working class in Bombay city in 1963 and recommended readjustments in the then existing series of the consumer price index. Prof. Lakdawala took his assignment relating to this subject with utmost seriousness and professional devotion. His recommendations were a landmark in the consumer price index construction which benefitted the workers, wage and salary earners in government and other establishments in the country enormously.

In 1989 the trade unions of Bombay approached the Institute of Social Sciences to look into the implementation of the 1982 New Consumer Price Index Series which severely affected the working class in the city. It was affected to the extent of finding a reduction in its Dearness Allowance (DA) of, on an average, between 50 and 150 rupees per month. I rushed to Ahmedabad, told Prof. Lakdawala about the request from the Bombay workers and had a long discussion with him about this problem. He took a keen personal interest in the matter and suggested a study design. The result was our publication: *New Consumer Price Index Series and the Bombay Working Class 1989*, released in 1990. Looking back, I can say that it was a significant intervention in the construction of a more realistic consumer price index for industrial workers and, thus, in getting the workers a just deal. The report was prepared by Prof. L. K.

Deshpande of the Economics Department, Bombay University, under Prof. Lakdawala's guidance. Incidentally, Prof. Deshpande was his student.

The second aspect I want to draw attention to is Prof. Lakdawala's commitment to decentralised planning.

Although Dr. Lakdawala's specialization was public finance and fiscal policy, his wide area of interests included planning. He brought a new emphasis to Indian planning through conditionalising the growth rate with the proviso of reduction in the proportion of people below the poverty line.

In Prof. Lakdawala we had an advocate for decentralised planning. At the Institute of Social Sciences, Dr. Lakdawala encouraged and helped chart research studies in political and economic decentralisation. Our projects on local government, decentralisation and Panchayati Raj are the result of this direction we received from Prof. Lakdawala. He had contributed a chapter "Decentralisation of Economic Power", in one of the earliest publications of the Institute: *Panchayati Raj in Karnataka Today: Its National Dimensions*, in which he had underlined the fact that "the logic of decentralisation is so powerful that it has been almost universally accepted ... since local resources are to be harnessed, local needs to be consulted, and local knowledge is needed, decentralisation is essential for the success of developmental efforts." Then, true to Lakdawala's concern for the ordinary people and development, he argued that decentralised planning is especially crucial "for those developmental efforts which aim at transforming the lives of the people or where the masses are involved". About decentralisation below state level he wrote: "It is no use transferring functions and powers unless we also transfer the wherewithals with which to discharge these functions".

We would like to continue with greater emphasis the research and studies on decentralised planning at the Institute of Social Sciences, along with our nation-wide studies on Panchayati Raj. It would be eminently fitting to establish a chair on decentralised planning at the Institute. My desire to have either a chair or an annual lecture series in memory of Prof. Lakdawala, expressed in my welcome speech at the symposium, has been fulfilled. The Planning Commission has instituted the D. T. Lakdawala Memorial Annual Lecture Series at the Institute of Social Sciences, beginning 1993, as a mark of respect for Prof. Lakdawala's long association with it. Eminent economists from our country and abroad will be invited every year.

We were fortunate to have five outstanding persons from the world of academics and politics who spoke on "Decentralised Planning". All of them knew Prof. Lakdawala and they shared his concerns for meaningful planning processes, interests of the working class and, above all, society at large.

George Mathew

Director
Institute of Social Sciences

1

Malcolm S. Adiseshiah

TOWARDS MEANINGFUL DECENTRALISED PLANNING

THIS symposium on Decentralised Planning commemorates our dear friend, guide and colleague, Prof. D T Lakdawala. It is appropriate that on this memorable occasion and on this subject, I recall his advice on decentralised planning at the 1983 Bangalore seminar on Centre-State Relations. His advice was that "it must be recognised that decentralisation is only a means; the end is people-oriented planning. Decentralisation is only a starting point to this end in the hope that the effective organisation of the people meant to bring them in the production process can be more successful at the lower points. There is a fear based on past experience that at lower levels the vested interests are more powerful. This apprehension must be proved false if decentralisation is to hold the field."

When in 1989 the new government headed by the Janata Dal had been voted to power, in its approach to the Eighth Five Year Plan (Towards Social Transformation: Approach to the VIII Five Year Plan, 1990-1995, Planning Commission, May 1990) it

Presidential Address.

declared that democratic decentralisation covering both political and economic processes will require political will.

We have now talked about decentralised planning for nearly half a century – from the First Five Year Plan (1950-55) onwards. Our actions, however, seem to move in the contrary direction. For instance, in agriculture which is actually a state subject, the union's plan share in 1991-92 was 39 per cent of total plan resources; in village and small industries, another state subject, the union share was 46.47 per cent; in rural development it was 54.02 per cent; in social and women's welfare it was 79.02 per cent and in family welfare it was 100 per cent. The situation vis-a-vis decentralisation of powers and finances below the state level, involving local bodies – panchayats, municipal councils and municipal corporations – is even worse. They have no powers even in areas which are clearly within their competence and are their responsibility, like primary schools, primary health centres and sub-centres. Local bodies are being starved of funds where generous grants and equitable tax sharing are inescapable. The Ashok Mehta Committee, for instance, had estimated that if the state plan expenditures and non-plan development expenditure allocable to districts in 1977-78 had been spent through Panchayati Raj institutions, it would have amounted to Rs. 8 crores per district (with an average of four Panchayat councils), on which a further Rs. 8 crores could have been raised from banks and other sources.

Now what could be done to make decentralised planning real and effective? I suggest two basic measures and stop there, leaving it to the other participants to elaborate on them. The two measures are: first, regular periodic elections to the local bodies – the three-tier Panchayati Raj institutions – recommended by the Balwantrai Mehta study team and the Ashok Mehta Committee; and second, agrarian reform. The two are inter-related and should be acted upon simultaneously.

The first measure is to hold periodic elections at the panchayat level as a means of involving people in the village in their developmental activities. This is against the top-down philosophy which we have inherited and which we have been practising since the days of the First Plan and which has resulted in the panchayat elections not being held for some or all the three-tiers for 10 years in most states. Way back in 1952, Nehru warned that though we had to start with the top-down approach in the first plan, soon we had to develop a procedure whereby "people may feel that the plan is something that has been evolved with their cooperation, so that they are responsible for its success". After two general elections, he realised that democracy with universal adult franchise does not throw up a pro-poor government. Looking around Parliament, he saw that instead of small farmers and landless labourers, who constitute 90 per cent of the rural people, being elected through adult suffrage, the elected representatives were well-to-do, large and medium farmers.

The second measure is to ensure that the proposed periodic panchayat elections do not simply transfer power from the states' well-to-do elites to the rich elites at the district and village levels. The

RBI's all India Debt and Investment Surveys over three decades, 1961, 1971 and 1981, show the skewed rural assets distribution, with the bottom 39 per cent of rural households owning only 5 per cent of all assets, while the top 5 per cent own 46 per cent. The National Sample Survey (NSS) and the Agricultural Census report higher proportions of marginal land holdings and landless labour households. In such a situation, holding panchayat elections would benefit the well-to-do farmers. In the case of Karnataka, for example, the Zilla Parishad elected chairmen (Adhyakshas) were 33.3 per cent Lingayats owning 20 to 100 acres of land each and 22.2 per cent Vokkligas owning 20-40 acres each. This contrasts with West Bengal where, first, land reforms were carried out, with the result that of the total 46,000 elected members of the three-tier panchayati structure, 75 per cent of the chairmen and members were small and marginal farmers.

The problem faced by the country, which accounts for the major part of its maldevelopment, is expressed in massive poverty, increasing unemployment, growing inequality, along with dismally low human development indices in terms of literacy, life expectancy, infant mortality, safe drinking water, rural infrastructure, natural resource protection etc. What is required today is self-sustained development. It is proposed to make the Panchayati Raj institutions responsible for drawing up realistic plans, of which the state and national plans will be the aggregate. The panchayat institutions will then be the willing and effective executors of the plan that they have formulated.

But simply bringing planning down to the state

and panchayat levels will not solve the above problems faced by the country. The history of the country's development shows that all measures to tackle poverty, generate employment (except for the Maharashtra Employment Guarantee Scheme), and promote a more equitable socio-economic order through the Integrated Rural Development Programme (IRDP), National Rural Employment Programme (NREP), Jawahar Rozgar Yojna (JRY), Self-Employment Programme for Urban Poor (SEPUP), Drought Prone Areas Programme (DPAP), Small Farmers Development Agency (SFDA), Marginal Farmers and Landless Labourers Agency (MFLA), and land reforms, have all emanated from the union. The states have been allergic to these development programmes. Does this point to the validity of what Prof. Lakdawala called "cooperative federalism", which is expressed through the Planning Commission, National Development Council, the Inter-State Council and some of the centrally sponsored schemes?

He explained "cooperative federalism" thus: while planned economic development demanded central initiative, action, supervision and coordination in many spheres, it also demanded state assistance, help and intelligent cooperation in the achievement of national objectives and administration of central regulations and rules. The great diversities in circumstances and detailed needs necessitated state adaptation of national programmes and wide experimentation. The plans increasingly became more detailed, and national targets were broken into state and area targets, group targets, and even family targets, which could be achieved only by the enthusiastic responses of the state and local bodies.

Not a unitary state but federalism; federalisation of a slightly different sort from the traditional one, "cooperative federalism", became imperative. This need found expression in the institutions of the Planning Commission (with its five-year and annual plan discussions) and the National Development Council.

2

Pranab Mukherjee

PANCHAYATI RAJ: A PREREQUISITE FOR DECENTRALISED PLANNING

PROF. Adiseshiah, Shri Hegde, Shri George Fernandes, Dr. Ashim Dasgupta, Dr. Mathew, and friends, at the very outset let me express my gratitude to the Institute for inviting me to inaugurate and participate in this timely symposium on "Decentralised Planning" to honour the memory of Prof. D. T. Lakdawala.

Dr. Lakdawala was an outstanding personality who, not only in his official capacity as Deputy Chairman of the Planning Commission but also through his forthright personal views and very strong conceptual clarity, guided us on several important matters affecting the life of the people at large.

While introducing the subject of today's discussion, the Director of the Institute of Social Sciences made a very pertinent suggestion, that of instituting a chair or an annual lecture series in memory of Dr. Lakdawala in an appropriate institution or university. From the Planning Commission's side, I fully support the proposal and we will examine how we can help in the matter.

Inaugural Address

The subject of decentralisation of the planning process was very dear to Prof. Lakdawala. While we have made some moves in that direction, frankly, I would like to admit that beyond these we have not been able to make much headway. In the earlier plan periods, though we talked of people's participation and tried to provide some sort of institutional support, for instance, an organization like the Bharat Sevak Samaj was created at the initiative of the then Deputy Chairman of the Planning Commission and Planning Minister, Shri Gulzari Lal Nanda, neither the involvement of the people nor the decentralisation of planning – in the formulation as well as implementation stages – came about in any significant manner.

In the eighties, experiments in effective local self-government or Panchayati Raj were initiated in a few states like Karnataka, Kerala and West Bengal, but these have failed to generate a snowballing effect and large parts of the country continue to be characterized by a political vacuum, in institutional terms, below the state level. In some areas; even the people's institutions like panchayats or other non-governmental agencies are simply non-existent, thereby making the task of translating the concept of decentralised planning into a practical reality all the more daunting.

Keeping in view the experiences we have gathered through the Panchayati Raj system in certain states I have just mentioned, the approach adopted in the Eighth Five-Year Plan envisages similar pilot experiments in about 150 blocks. To my mind, however, the time has come, today, when much more is needed to be done. Any serious consideration of decentralisation of planning requires the strengthening and revitalization of democratic institutions themselves.

What strikes me in this context is the increasing distance between the elected and the electors. If I remember correctly, in the last Lok Sabha elections there were 540 million electors and the total number elected to the Lok Sabha were about 540. That means, on an average, one million electors are electing one representative to the sovereign Parliament. And assuming safely that there will be no delimitation as per the constitutional provision till 2000 A.D., by the turn of the century almost 700 million electors would be electing 540 Members of Parliament. If we are talking of strengthening democratic institutions and electoral reforms, particularly the elimination of money power and muscle power, how is this possible if the number of electors is so high?

In my view, the time has come when we should switch over from the present two-tier system of government to a three-tier system comprising the centre, the states and block panchayats. Instead of having one Parliament and 25 state assemblies, we could have 5,000 block parliaments and entrust the entire local administration and development to these block parliaments which would be accountable to the people at the block level. The number of electors with respect to each block parliament would be far less and, hence, transparency and visibility in the system far greater.

Minor irrigation, primary education – even secondary education – law, judiciary, normal enforcement of law, agriculture, animal husbandry, dairy, afforestation, health and family planning, the whole gamut of rural activities, could be initiated at the block level, or even below, at the village level, and could be terminated at the block level.

Now, when we talk of decentralisation, it does not merely imply that planning decisions are taken at below district or below block level. Surely, if a block plan is worked out by a block development officer (BDO) or by a *mukhia* who has been elected 10 or 15 years ago and is no longer accountable to the people, that does not constitute decentralised planning. I do not believe that merely by transferring the decision-making process to a lower level, the local level, we can achieve the objective of decentralisation. Effective decentralisation requires the necessary decentralised institutional arrangements at various levels.

Yes, non-governmental organisations (NGOs) can play a major role in strengthening the roots of the institutions. At the same time, however, we shall have to keep in view the limitations of these organisations. In this country, if you look at the success stories with regard to the NGOs you will find that, by and large, these have emerged around outstanding personalities. One Anna Hazare or one R. K. Misra can create an organisation and motivate people to do very good work. But these cannot serve as substitutes for institutional arrangements, which is what is required if we are to begin the process of decentralised planning and development in any meaningful way. In this context, I am happy to note that the Institute of Social Sciences has undertaken the task of studying and surveying the status of local self-government, Panchayati Raj, in the country, covering a large number of states. We, in the Planning Commission, definitely look forward to the findings of these studies.

It has also become fairly apparent that in our system, institutional arrangements cannot be sustained in a viable manner without constitutional guarantees. If we want our local bodies, whether panchayats or nagar palikas, to deliver the goods, is it not time that they be provided with adequate muscle? Which means that not only they should have the authority to take decisions, at the same time they should also be assured of access to adequate resources. They should have some sort of constitutional safety which will ensure that they are not at the mercy of the whims and caprices of the government of the day.

Coming to the actual planning process we have noticed that we are trying to do too many things, with too many agencies involved and, therefore, thinly spreading our resources in human, material and financial terms. As a result there is a big gap between our objectives and our actual achievements.

Now if we have a decentralised institutional arrangement which is visible, distinguishable, which has transparency and at the same time if we can integrate all the apparatus, all the resources available, then perhaps it would be easier to implement things.

I will not mention the name of a district but both Mr. Hegde and Dr. Dasgupta may be aware of it. Recently, I was going through the district planning documents of a particular district and I found that to implement a developmental outlay of Rs 8 crores in a year, the actual establishment cost is more than Rs 16 crores. What type of planning is possible in such a situation? And in certain areas, I noticed, in that district, at the village level, at the lowest level, there are as many as 26 functionaries either fully or partly belonging to both sets of government, state and central. And none of them are fully engaged. Now how to coordinate these things and have an integrated approach. And if we had that, perhaps with much less cost we could have achieved much more. So decentralisation of planning, to my mind, is not merely a cliche or slogan, it is an urgent necessity. From our experiences we have found that we cannot achieve some of our targets in the areas of afforestation, literacy and population control. The involvement of people is the key to the success of these programmes. And surely, the involvement of the people is not possible through the bureaucratic apparatus.

From my own experiences, I can tell you, and perhaps Dr. Dasgupta will bear me out, that without involving people in large numbers very little is achieved. I started, before I joined politics or Parliament, as a teacher. I set up a small organisation for eradication of illiteracy in the late '60s with the blessings of the then Calcutta University Vice-Chancellor, Dr. Sen. And we soon realised that unless we can convert the slogan of literacy into some sort of mass movement, mass participation, simply by investing in education and debating whether 6 per cent of the GDP should be diverted for education or not, is not going to help us. Even an investment of 12 per cent, in terms of GDP, in education will not eradicate illiteracy unless you can back that up with a mass movement for literacy.

Today, in some of the districts that are declaring themselves totally literate, mass participation and mass involvement is there in a big way, and without mass involvement, total literacy could not have been achieved. These are also districts where local bodies, panchayats, have a considerable if not vibrant presence.

The idea I am putting forward, to be given some thought by a distinguished gathering like the one present here, is that we should have a regular constitutional provision[1] to secure effective decentralisation of powers. When I suggest this, I know very well there are other constitutional limitations like the Supreme Court judgements, basic structure of the Constitution etc. I am not going into those aspects. All I am suggesting and arguing for is that if there is a strong public opinion, if there is a strong people's desire that in order to support the democratic structure we require decentralisation, we require adequate constitutional arrangements backed by constitutional amendments at some point of time, these could get reflected in the normal process of the functioning. Without strengthening, safeguarding and making effective the functioning of local self-government, it will be extremely difficult to translate the idea of decentralisation into a reality. Even increasing the number of Members of Parliament from 500 to 1000 is not going to help. Neither would the splitting of states into smaller ones, the enlarging of the state list nor reducing the union list.

What is required is a structural arrangement with

some uniformity that includes a third tier of government, which also keeps in view the diversity prevailing in the socio-economic conditions across the country. This, to my mind, gets adequately reflected in the Panchayati Raj system. These institutions can become the effective instruments of decentralisation of the planning process, of economic planning and of economic development, of which Dr. Lakdawala was an ardent advocate.

NOTE

1. The 73rd and 74th Constitution Amendment Bills giving constitutional status to panchayats and municipal bodies was passed by Lok Sabha on 22 December, 1992 and the Rajya Sabha on 23 December, 1992. It received President's assent on 20 April, 1993 and became part of the Constitution from 24 April, 1993.

3

Ramakrishna Hegde

LOCAL SELF-GOVERNMENT IN KARNATAKA: PLANNING FROM BELOW

MR. Chairman and friends, I am beholden to the Institute of Social Sciences, and particularly to Dr. George Mathew, for giving me an opportunity to participate in this symposium which has been organised to commemorate the services rendered by an illustrious son of our country, Prof. Lakdawala. He was a doyen, not only in the field of economics but also in the field of social planning. It is appropriate that George Mathew has proposed instituting a chair in Prof. Lakdawala's name at the Institute of Social Sciences itself. I hope Pranab Mukherjee will fulfil his promise.

You have just heard two learned speeches, one by the Deputy Chairman of the Planning Commission, Pranab Mukherjee, and the other by the Chairman of this symposium, Prof. Adiseshiah. I have to say something about certain remarks made by Pranab Mukherjee and also by Adiseshiah in regard to the Karnataka experiment, but I will do it a little later.

Unfortunately, during the last twenty years or so democracy in our country has been reduced to a government *for* the people – or at least it was claimed so. People hardly have any role in shaping their own destinies at various levels, which has meant democracy in a very limited sense. It was Panditji who started the Community Development Programme way back in the 1950s. And later on another scheme was added to that which was the Panchayati Raj system. Jawaharlal Nehru was very keen that at the grassroots level we must have institutions which made participatory democracy a reality. Such participatory democracy meant people's participation not only in the administration of the local institutions, but also in preparing plans and schemes for the development of their respective areas and supervising the execution of such plans and schemes. Otherwise it had little meaning.

I was shocked a few years ago when the then Prime Minister, Rajiv Gandhi, started having meetings with the District Magistrates of different states to discuss the planning process and the execution of district plans. And later on, the Prime Minister called a conference of the Chief Secretaries of different states to discuss the same subject. I protested against this procedure. The Chief Secretaries of the states had absolutely no knowledge. And this was done over the heads of the Chief Ministers of the states.

Over the years, the Government of India and the Planning Commission started schemes which were known as "centrally sponsored schemes". I can understand "central schemes" and that also to a limited extent. There are central universities. And there are central research institutions. This I can understand. But I could not understand what they actually meant by centrally sponsored schemes for the people of this country.

What we want today are village sponsored schemes, people sponsored schemes. If people, here in Delhi, think that all the wisdom is concentrated in the offices of the central government and the Planning Commission, they are totally wrong. The apprehensions that were expressed about the malpractices in the panchayat and zilla parishad elections are no more justified than the apprehensions regarding the state assembly elections and parliamentary elections. If at all, such malpractices are very infrequent and on a reduced scale because the constituencies are small, the people are known to each other and there is not much play of money and muscle power.

It might be true that sometimes at the local level, petty politics comes into play. But we have to face it. In Karnataka, in 1985, we introduced a revolutionary legislation called Zilla Parishad, Mandal Panchayat and Nyaya Panchayat Act. We passed this legislation towards the end of 1983 but the central government did not give its assent for over one-and-a-half years. Some of the legislators had to go and observe *dharna* outside the Raj Bhavan, where the President of India was staying during his visit to Bangalore. Only then this legislation received his assent.

Mr. Pranab Mukherjee gave an instance – he did not reveal the name of the district – where the total plan outlay provided for district development was Rs. 8 crores and the total establishment expenditure was Rs. 16 crores. This has not been the experience of Karnataka. In Karnataka both the execution as well as the formulation of district plans were left to the district bodies and Mandal Panchayats. And the total administrative expenditure, to give you one instance in a district, was Rs. 4 crores as against Rs. 25 crores provided for development. I am giving you the instance of Bangalore district.

One unique thing about the Karnataka legislation is that the Gram Sabha in every village, in every Mandal Panchayat, was given a statutory status. A Gram Sabha must meet at least once in six months and every member of the Mandal Panchayat, every official functionary and every office bearer, the president, vice-president, etc., must be present on that occasion; it is compulsory. All the voters are the members of Gram Sabha, that is, everybody who is above the age of 18. And everyone has the complete freedom to ask questions, criticise and attack, if necessary, the functioning and performance of the Mandal Panchayat. This has been a very healthy practice. Do you know the result? In several mandals corruption cases came to light in meetings of the Gram Sabhas. In the district of Shimoga, in a particular Mandal Panchayat, in the first year after it was elected, the sale of fishing rights for a particular water tank amounted to Rs. 75,000. Prior to that, for years when the fisheries department auctioned the rights, the proceeds had amounted to not more than Rs. 12,000. In the very first year, because this was done under the supervision, under the vigilant eyes of the representatives of the people, there was such an enormous increase in the revenue. And under the Act, the Mandal Panchayat is totally entitled to this income.

The second year the president of the Mandal Panchayat wanted to be smart. He somehow got a resolution passed in the Mandal Panchayat authorising him to negotiate. After some time, he sold the rights to somebody else and reported to the Mandal Panchayat in the next meeting that the sale of fishing rights that year had fetched one lakh and twenty thousand rupees (Rs. 1,20,000) as compared to Rs. 75,000 in the previous year. The members of the Mandal Panchayat accepted and approved of the sale. But in the next Gram Sabha meeting several people stood up and said that the president had sold the rights for Rs. 1,80,000 whereas he had reported to the Mandal Panchayat that it had fetched only Rs. 1,20,000. The president of the panchayat had to confess that it was true that the sale of fishing rights had fetched Rs. 1,80,000 and he made up the loss.

This has two lessons for us. First, corruption is less in a decentralised administration. Second, if the administration is conducted in as close proximity as possible to the people, there is very little scope for the guilty to escape. I shall give you one or two more instances to illustrate this point further.

In Karnataka, according to the Panchayat Act, a mandal means, if it is a very big village with more than 12,000 people, a village, otherwise a group of villages. All the government administrative functions at that level, whether it is primary education, construction of a village road, electricity supply, small irrigation works, drinking water supply, etc., are transferred to the Mandal Panchayat. Not only is the responsibility for carrying out these functions transferred, but also the resources provided in the state budget for these works are transferred.

In addition, there is a lump sum grant. There are three sources of revenue so far as the Zilla Parishad and the Mandal Panchayat are concerned. One is the plan funds. They are transferred along with the schemes. Second is the income of these institutions themselves. They may resort to various kinds of taxation, etc. And the third is allocation of lump sum grants. Certain criteria are fixed on the basis of which these lump sum grant are given, which I will elaborate in a moment. Therefore, the resources that are available at the grassroots level institution, the Mandal Panchayat, are adequate to discharge the responsibility of development and administration entrusted to that institution.

In Karnataka, we prepared a detailed scheme as to how the planning process should start from the basic body, that is, the Mandal Panchayat. I am not referring to what is going on now because the very first statement made by the Chief Minister after he was sworn in was that the new government will abolish the Zilla Parishads and Mandal Panchayats, which the government finally did. The planning was done from the bottom up. First, by the Mandal Panchayat and after that by the Zilla Parishad. After that the plans were sent to the state government. There has been some criticism that at the mandal level, people do not know how to prepare a plan for the development of that area. I do not agree with that. Yes, in the beginning, in the first year, everybody would like to add his own scheme with the result that the plan becomes a little too big from the point of view of availability of resources. But once the people realise that they have only so much resources and the plan has to be framed within the limitation of these resources, they do understand and conflicts are normally resolved. This was our experience.

We laid down an annual time-table for planning at every tier:

1. State government communicates the total outlay that is available for the annual plan of the Zilla Parishads (ZPs) and Mandals and asks ZPs to prepare composite district plans. That is in July.

2. ZPs communicate the outlays to Mandals based on certain criteria, in August. And in the same month, Mandals hold Gram Sabha meetings, finalise their plans, and send them to ZPs.

3. Next month, that is September, the ZPs prepares the district plans by integrating mandal plans with their own plans and sends these to the state government.

4. The government level meeting with ZPs, attended by heads of departments to finalise the plans, is held in October.

5. The sectoral outlays of state and district plans are integrated in each department and the state plan is finalised in November.

6. Draft state plan is discussed with the Planning Commission and finalised in January.

7. And after that, in February/March, the budget is passed.

The criteria on the basis of which the outlay, the outright or untied grant, is decided at the district level are as follows: population weightage, 50%; backwardness in agriculture, 5%; backwardness ir irrigation, 7%; backwardness as measured by the value of industrial output, 5%; backwardness in communications as measured by road and railway mileage per 100 sq. kms and per lakh of population, 5%; backwardness in financial infrastructure, 2%; backwardness in medical health facilities, 5%; backwardness in power supply, 5%; problems of the weaker sections (4% agricultural labour and others); special problems for *malnad* areas and drought prone areas, altogether 12%. And similarly, weighted criteria have been fixed for the distribution of the untied grant among the Mandal Panchayats – population, 50%; area of mandal, 15%; dry-land area, 15%; agricultural labour population, 10%; per capita resources raised (that is, as an incentive), 10%.

So far as Karnataka is concerned, it is not true that the administrative expenditure exceeds the total developmental outlay; far from it. As I told you, the Bangalore district spends hardly Rs. 4 crores on the administrative machinery, whereas its income – only the plan outlay, not other sources – is Rs. 20 to 25 crores.

It is my conviction that unless planning starts from below, it is not possible to have a people's plan. In Karnataka the experiment has been very successful. I do not say it was absolutely flawless. But it was a great experiment, a revolutionary step.

There were certain measures I wanted to take which I could not. Perhaps, with these measures the complaints that came later about internal fights, about misuse of office, etc., would have been absolutely minimal. The first was a training programme for the members of Mandal Panchayats and Zilla Parishads. These men and women had never tasted power in their lives as they did after the introduction of this measure. I will never forget in my whole life one spectacle when this experiment was inaugurated. The present Prime Minister was there as the chief guest, as also Mr. S. K. Dey – who can be called the father of community development in this country. In front of us, there were 60,000 people of which 19,000 were women. Some may ask, what is so great about the numbers? Sixty thousand is not so large a gathering. Here in Delhi, at the Boat Club there have been instances where 10 to 20 lakhs have gathered. In Bangalore, on that occasion, however, all the 60,000 present were elected representatives. Every one of them was a representative of the people. Never in human history had such a spectacle taken place.

There is reservation of 25% seats for women and 18% for Scheduled Castes/Scheduled Tribes. And wherever backward class candidates are not elected in adequate numbers, the Act provides for their nomination. That means all sections are represented. Karnataka has adopted a two-tier system which was more successful than the three-tier system which was tried earlier in the state. The panchayats and the Zilla Parishads should be the main centres of both development and planning. I think it was Pranab Mukherjee who has just said that due to malpractices the elections do not throw up the true representatives of the people. I am afraid I cannot agree. The Directive Principles of State Policy of the Constitution enjoins us that there should be local self-government, with adequate powers and resources provided to them.

Unfortunately, we have never implemented this. And during the last twenty years, even the existing local self-government structure has been totally destroyed.

In the end, I would like to emphasise that the district unit, what it is called, Zilla Parishad or District Council, should function as a district government. There is the central government, there is the state government. And at the district level there should be a district government. The district unit, however, should not have power to interfere in the mandal affairs, because the Mandal Panchayat should also be treated as a unit of government.

We have ensured that no Zilla Parishad or Mandal Panchayat is superseded. If there is maladministration, in exceptional circumstances, these bodies can be dissolved, in which case elections must be held within a period of six months. There were hundreds of local self-government institutions in Karnataka where elections had not been held for 10 to 15 years. After I became the Chief Minister, within five months, elections to all these bodies were conducted. I hope the present Deputy Chairman of the Planning Commission will do at least two things: first, give full scope to the district and panchayat bodies to formulate their own plans; and second, cut down totally the so-called centrally sponsored schemes. Centrally sponsored schemes mean treating all state governments as union territories. Except for schemes of national importance which would benefit all the states, none of the other schemes should be treated as centrally sponsored schemes. These schemes must come from the people themselves and they must be called village sponsored schemes.

4

Ashim Dasgupta

PANCHAYATI RAJ AND DECENTRALISED PLANNING IN WEST BENGAL

MR. Chairman Mr. Hegde, Mr. Fernandes, Dr. Mathew and friends, I am indeed thankful to the Institute of Social Sciences for inviting me to the symposium in honour of Prof. Lakdawala and on decentralised planning.

True to the concern of Prof. Lakdawala and also the theme of this symposium, may I, Mr. Chairman, with your concurrence, choose as the theme of my presentation, "Panchayati Raj and Decentralisation in Planning". At the risk of apparent over-simplification, I will choose to distinguish at the very outset between two possible scenarios relating to Panchayati Raj and decentralisation in planning.

Scenario I: We may, in this scenario, choose to accept the existing unequal distribution of land and other rural assets. The moment we accept this, we are actually accepting, by and large, the situation prevailing in the country as a whole – though there may be variations across states. Mr. Chairman, as per the latest available National Sample Survey (NSS) data for the country as a whole, the top 10 per cent of rural households own about 70 per cent of the agricultural land and the bottom 90 per cent, including small and marginal farmers, own the remaining 20 per cent; the bottom-most, the lowest decile do not own anything.

Suppose we accept this and then introduce Panchayati Raj and also introduce a scheme of decentralisation? You can introduce Panchayati Raj through legislation, through a constitutional amendment. But if there has not been any peasants' struggle for the land, in other words, if, therefore, it is the top 10 per cent of households in rural areas who dominate the decision making, then it is possible – I shall be very careful not to be deterministic – so it is quite likely that after the panchayat elections are held, the panchayat bodies may, directly or indirectly, though not necessarily, be dominated by these vested interests. This is one significant possibility.

You then allow a scheme of decentralisation, from the state headquarters down to the districts, to the blocks and below. Well, first of all, there certainly will be a disaggregation of schemes. Suppose that there is sufficient disaggregation of schemes and you come to the level of, not a district but a block, and through the block to the level of the village. I am just thinking of a possibility. Then, it is possible, in this village, that if 10 per cent of the population own – I am quoting the national average – 71 per cent of the land, then they are the people who are the major decision makers through their ownership of land, of the production process itself; they will decide where the irrigation projects will be installed, how the road alignment will be carved out to carry the produce, primarily out of their own fields, etc. It is possible that this vested interest group will have a decisive power. But even then, friends, it would be a scheme of decentralisation. You can put officials, and indeed, experts down to the level of blocks. And I have no hesitation in saying that this would be a more efficient system compared to the previous system, where you did not have even this kind of decentralisation.

You can have glossy booklets on district planning, block planning. These days you have a computerised system, you have the data-base, all right. You have all these things. But what you do not have is the involvement of the people. Because, after all, they are not the primary beneficiaries of the entire process because of their alienation from the land. There is no adequate material basis for their continuing involvement in the process. This will be Panchayati Raj and decentralisation without adequate involvement of the people. But even then, Mr. Chairman, I would be strongly in favour of this decentralisation and Panchayati Raj compared to the present situation. Because, first of all and most importantly, if you have devolved the so-called power down to that level, even that can become the rallying point for organisations of common people, when the time for election comes. And this by itself may help to ignite their aspirations for change. There will be a real conflict of interests. As a result, there will be two possible outcomes: one, a withdrawal from the process of decentralisation itself. It has happened in some states. But I am an incurable optimist. There is the other possibility. The common people will strike back and if they do that they will ask for land reform. If you do not start with land reforms, you could very well end with it. That takes me to scenario two.

Scenario II: Here, we begin by not accepting the existing unequal distribution of land. We begin with redistributive land reforms. Why begin with land reforms? We have NSS data across the states with respect to major crops as well as cropping intensity, which shows that the highest record of production per hectare is not obtained from the land of big farmers nor from the land of middle farmers but from the land of small and marginal farmers. Therefore, when you are redistributing land in favour of poorer farmers, you are basically maximising output because he is the most productive agent. Also, the highest employment generation occurs on their land, so you are also maximising employment.

Well, with modesty, Mr. Chairman, I shall just mention that in West Bengal, we started with land reforms. Not for any reason of charity but for reasons of productivity and employment generation, I just mentioned. And according to the same NSS data, again with modesty, I may point out that as against the national picture where small and marginal farmers own around 29 per cent of the land, in West Bengal, after certain steps have been taken towards land reforms, now, small and marginal farmers own about 60 per cent of total agricultural land. And to this, if we add the land under the operational control of recorded *bargadars*, whom you cannot evict, then the total percentage of agricultural land over which the poorer farmers have effective control, either through ownership or permanent operational control, will exceed 75 per cent at present.

Now I would again point out, that these efforts

towards land reforms were not products of any legislative action. Land reform legislations have been there since the early fifties, but there were no land reforms in the fifties. I have this cynical view regarding the constitutional amendment also. I agree with your view also Mr. Chairman, – if you have the political will you change things but if you do not, then no amount of legislative tinkering will help.

So it was not legislation. It was basically the peasants' movement, organised peasants' movement, as a part of the left and democratic movement in the state and other parts of the country, that brought about land reforms. And after the land reforms – well, there is a long history that I am cutting short – when the Left Front government came to power in 1977, a decision was taken, in June 1978, to hold elections to the panchayats.

There is a three-tier panchayat system in West Bengal. You have the Zilla Parishad at the district level, 17 districts in all, with I think 678 members. Then at the block level, you have 339 blocks and therefore, the total number of Panchayat Samiti elected members would be a little more than 5,000. And then the Gram Panchayats – totalling 3,305 – whose total number of members would be around 55,000. But I should point out, the *anchal* is not exactly a village but a cluster of 10 villages, on an average.

After the panchayat elections were held, we took a profile of the so-called class background of the elected representatives: 75 per cent of them came from the categories of small and marginal farmers and below. This basically tallies with what was said regarding the share of small and marginal farmers in effective control over land. At the gram panchayat level, it is slightly higher, but on the whole that is the picture. Between 75 to 80 per cent of the elected representatives at the gram panchayat level came from the categories of small and marginal farmers, landless agricultural labourers, poor artisans, and so forth.

There was a change in the correlation of forces with respect to the political structure at the village level – this was not a magical thing, not an accident. It was because of this continued economic struggle, even prior to the panchayat elections.

Planning Objectives

It is very important, before we talk about decentralisation and involvement of people through panchayats, to talk about the priorities of planning itself. It is not simply land reforms. It does not help to give just a parcel of land to a poor farmer – he may not be able to retain it. Or to merely ensure tenurial security. He will have to be immediately provided with non-land inputs, the most important of which is irrigation, an assured supply of irrigation water. In irrigation, of course, there is the crucial choice of technology. From big dams and big tubewells to tube wells with submersible pump-sets, shallow tubewells with centrifugal pump-sets, down to dug wells, you have an entire spectrum of technology choices.

In seeds, it would not do to just say that we want high yielding varieties. There is an entire spectrum from which you have to carefully choose. There is a middle-yielding variety which is just correct, given the local conditions. There is choice regarding fertilizers as well, an appropriate mix of chemical and bio-fertilisers, and choice relating to cropping patterns. Next, there is choice relating to land use. Not all lands are suitable for crop cultivation. Highlands in several districts may have to be used for fodder cultivation, and there is a need for integration with social forestry. Finally, industry often grows out of the womb of agriculture – industries related to agriculture, industries for supplying agricultural inputs as well as for processing agricultural products. So there is also choice regarding the mix of agriculture and industry. And once you have this overall view, then comes the need for marketing and, therefore, road development as part of the entire package. And once these marketing centres come up they become the decentralised urban centres. Decentralised urban planning becomes a part of this strategy of decentralisation in rural areas.

In this entire view I would not pick out too many things. I would certainly pick out one thing which relates to choice of technology. Now, we in West Bengal have insisted that the technology to be chosen will have to be that which would make fuller use of local labour and local resources. It will have to be not only labour intensive but local resource intensive and also improved – it is possible to have such technology. The technology will have to be, I shall use the word, divisible. I put emphasis on this because if the technology is lumpy, it results in a big project which cannot be decentralised. Decision making, then, for technological reasons will have to be centralised. Whenever you have a choice, and if you are serious about decentralisation, very often, consciously, you have to opt for a divisible technology. In our experience, sometimes such technology also has the highest social benefit-cost ratio. In irrigation we have seen this.

Now, with this class background of the panchayats and with this objective of planning, we started giving panchayats certain powers. Not too many powers all at once. There is need for ground level testing of ourselves. Those were the days you would recall, Mr. Chairman, Mr. Hegde, when the Food for Work Programme was initiated. It is a wage-based programme which later on was called National Rural Employment Programme (NREP) and now it is called Jawahar Rozgar Yojana (JRY). The other programme was the Integrated Rural Development Programme (IRDP). The first is the wage employment programme, the second, the self-employment, subsidy and bank loan programme.

Now, I chose this because our experience has been slightly different in the two cases and for good reasons. We gave panchayats the power of implementation, *they* became our implementing agencies. Not for too many schemes, just these two schemes to begin with – Food for Work and IRDP.

In IRDP we did not succeed, to begin with. We asked panchayats to do one thing very seriously – you choose your beneficiaries. IRDP is a target group-oriented scheme in which big farmers cannot enter and the small and marginal farmers have to be chosen very carefully. And some of the studies carried out by the Ministry of Rural Development indicate that for the state of West Bengal the choice of beneficiaries has been 100 per cent correct. And that became our problem. Banks were reluctant to give loans to very poor farmers.

Banks are a collateral-based institution and there was, the term I use, "indivisibility" on the bankers' side. There was not adequate divisibility. Banks were asking for few, high loan accounts. Few accounts but big accounts. That is what they are used to. We were asking for many, but small accounts. We were asking for a divisible reaction on the part of bankers; like in the case of technology. But banks were not prepared for it. We did not succeed with our ideas, but we did in this manner – if bankers do not have divisibility, our system will provide the divisibility. We asked the panchayats: if the banks cannot collect the loans, can you, panchayats, collect loans? People talk about loan melas, we actually organised repayment melas. And we did some work for the banks. Eventually, we could cross the hump, this hurdle. I will not elaborate more except to mention how panchayats fared in respect of the Food for Work Programme and NREP. I shall just mention an example. Incidentally, I am mightily surprised about the district Mr. Mukherjee was referring to. It is my business to know the details of the expenditure pattern for the 17 districts and 339 blocks in my state. I cannot recall any district with such expenditures. But Mr. Mukherjee mentioned that it is a district or area which three of us know; so, if Mr. Hegde does not know of this being in Karnataka and I do not know of this being in West Bengal, then, there is only one place which three of us know – that is the Union Territory of Delhi. This is very possible.

I have, however, in my mind, since reference was made to a district, a very disadvantaged district of the state, Purulia, which borders Bengal and Bihar. It is a drought-prone area with laterite soils. May I, Mr. Chairman, through you, invite all of you to visit West Bengal sometime. Do not believe me, my words. You choose wherever you want to go and go on your own. If you need any help from the government, let us know. Otherwise, you can find out for yourself.

Purulia is also a very picturesque district. There is a hill called Ayodhya Hills and should you like to take time off, you are most welcome to visit these hills. Now, close to that picturesque spot there is a block called Kashipur and the Darakeshwari river – a very typical Chotanagpur plateau river – flows through that block. A causeway, a small bridge, had to be constructed across the river. We asked a conventional government department what would be the estimated cost and the time required. They said that they would require two working seasons and Rs. 21 lakhs. Now, we did not have that much of money, nor could we wait that long. We then asked the panchayat, in this case the Panchayat Samiti at the block level, can you do the job? Incidentally, I did not mention that we give technical help to the panchayats, provide surveyors and engineers along with the usual administrative help.

The Panchayat Samiti took a few days to decide. We put only one condition to them: no hiring of contractors. They would have to directly implement the work by involving people and using the technical assistance they already had. The panchayat decided to implement the work by totally involving the local people. That bridge got constructed, not in two years, but in one year. Not with twenty-one lakh rupees but with six lakh rupees and with the same technical specifications. This is the order of economy of cost. I totally agree with Mr. Hegde when he says how economical it is when you decentralise. These days it is fashionable to hire consultants, sometimes from outside, to tell you how to economise. We don't need to do that. If we decentralise, we make the system accountable to people, that would bring about a sea change.

The Purulia experiment, apart from economising costs, was an experiment in involving people. The bridge that got constructed was not an engineering bridge alone, it was also a symbol of the people's love. This is the positive aspect, but I should immediately tell you the shortcomings which we recognised. There is a problem of dualism. The Public Works Department (PWD) also constructs roads, so there has to be coordination between the panchayat-run schemes and department-run schemes and also between the departments themselves. There is always the need for cooperation between, let us say, minor irrigation and irrigation waterways, between the entire irrigation department and the agriculture department. Not only is there a need for coordination but need for *decentralised coordination.* For this we initiated an experiment, I recall, back in 1983-84.

Organisational Structure

Somehow or other, and I place it before you for consideration, we realised that not simply the elected panchayat members, but also the officials and technical experts, will have to be brought together. So at the district level we then set up a district planning committee. And at the block level, a block planning committee. There was a long internal debate before we accepted the form. You see, we are all aware of the bureaucrat-technocrat controversy. We also know who will probably take leadership at that level. We are also aware about the problem of MPs and MLAs versus panchayat representatives. Any state which has experienced all this must have resolved it in one way or another. Now how did we go about it, or try to go about it?

With respect to the district planning committee, the Zilla Parishad *Sabhadhipati*, ZP chairman, is the chairman of the committee. But we made the District Magistrate the member-secretary. And on the one side the elected members of the Zilla Parishad, the Chiefs of the standing committees of the Zilla Parishads, six or seven, and all Panchayat Samiti – the block level panchayat – chairpersons are brought together. So this is the elected part of it. The official part includes the district level officers of all the concerned departments plus the banks' representatives. So these are the components of the district planning committee.

In this scenario what would be the place of the MLAs and MPs? Now, we had set up – I would like to know how this was resolved in Karnataka – over and above this district planning committee, a district planning coordination council which is a kind of general deliberative body, of which the district planning committee was the executive arm. The district planning coordination council comprised the district planning committee plus the MLAs and MPs. The council meets once in a while, but it is the district planning committee which is the executive, operative arm.

At the block level we have a block planning committee. The same model operates. Here the Panchayat Samiti Sabhapati, the block panchayat chief, is the chairperson and the Block Development Officer (BDO) is the Member-Secretary. In this committee the chiefs of the standing committees of the Panchayat Samiti are members and also the Gram Panchayat Pradhans are brought up and made members. And the block level officials constitute the official component of the committee. So this is as far as the organisational structure of decentralised planning is concerned.

Next, the funding pattern and then the implementation.

Financing

We realised – it seems our experience tallies with Karnataka's – that we had to make a distinction in the plan budget for each of the 44 departments. We introduced two categories in 1983 which have continued from then on, one the state level schemes and the other the district or below level schemes.

Any scheme which encompasses more than one district cannot be settled at the level of a district. It becomes a state level scheme. Schemes which are at the district or below, become district level schemes. In the road sector, for instance, state highways, of course, is a state level scheme. But district roads is a district subject. Similarly, if there is a village road which begins and ends within a block it becomes a block level subject.

When the budget is presented for each department for approval there is a clear separation between state level and district or below level schemes. We tried and we eventually have decentralised in terms of financial allocation. A little more than 50 per cent of the entire state budget is devolved down to district or below even as regards *decision making* about allocations. In fact – I was just comparing the figures – on an average, a district of West Bengal will have, in a good year, Rs 40-45 crores of plan budget for its own decision making. If a decision is taken at the block or district level no finance minister in West Bengal can say no to that.

After this delegation, the district knows what are the schemes under its jurisdiction, the funds are indicated in advance, and the district planning committee meets. And from the total funds received at the district level, by and large, about 70-75 per cent of the fund will be given to the block planning committee for distribution across the blocks, on the basis of certain criteria. When the fund comes to the block planning committee, apart from checking the technical aspects – for instance, what is the ground water position (there is a ground water mapping of the state down to the block level), what is the soil composition, etc. – which should accompany the plan, the *priorities* at the block and village level have to be reflected.

Kindly contrast this with scenario one. The fund comes to the level of the block. In the block planning committee the panchayat pradhans go back to their own *anchals* where they meet with representatives from each village. So, at the block planning committee meeting the plan that is initially formulated is not a plan of a few panchayat representatives. Then they have to go back again to their village and again hold a meeting – two meetings are mandatory in terms of the Panchayat Act of West Bengal per year. One is when the panchayat representative holds an open mass meeting to decide on the priorities of the village. And these priorities he brings to his discussion at the block planning committee. This is the most crucial point. If the planning exercise was limited to panchayat representatives, no matter what their class background, even if they come from a poorer class background they cease to represent the people. Discipline and internal monitoring are the crucial aspects of decentralised planning. And this is where I certainly agree with the point Mr. Hegde made and I have no hesitation in making it here again – along with the official instructions and so forth we had to give our own political organisational instructions day in and day out. Because otherwise there can be a relapse, a return to old ways of functioning. This point is very important. And I also have no hesitation in mentioning that the experience of the 17 districts varied. There is variation across the districts and also variation within the districts.

Where decentralised planning process was effective, the people's priorities got reflected in the block plan, whether it was in the choice of irrigation projects, their location, alignment of roads, everything.

You see, these block planning committee meetings could go on sometimes for sixteen hours. I could attend some of them as then I was not a minister, but in another capacity. These meetings were extremely interesting and also revealed how the conflicts were resolved. When we resolved them, we introduced a very small technique. And it is very interesting how quickly the panchayat functionaries could pick it up, at a pace which the M.A. Economics students in Calcutta University would also appreciate. It is just a two-way table. Take a sector like roads. Suppose in all, 20 road schemes are agreed upon. And you show the alignment, you show the quarterly targets for the job you want to do. Then, on top of it you have to indicate the source of funds. Maybe the first road is out of PWD funds, the second road may still be out of PWD funds but the third, fourth and fifth road may be out of Food for Work or NREP funds, now from the Jawahar Rozgar Yojana funds. We also have an untied fund, we call it district plan fund, and the last three may be from that source. So you have a two-way table, a two-by-two matrix, so to say. Just by looking at that you can see whether there is coordination or not. If there are too many zeros that would immediately indicate, that people have not put their heads together to adequately tap all the potential sources. But if the table is full, it means they have applied their minds, they have combined all resources to have a very coordinated plan. This is how the block plan, out of people's priorities, technical things, financial considerations, is framed. And this block plan is sent then to the district level. Block plans plus block level proposals of inter-block schemes are relevant for planning at the district level.

Integration at the district level is a very interesting exercise. It is not simply arithmetical addition of block plans. Normally, block plans once proposed cannot be ruled out by the district planning committee unless there is a gross violation of priorities. Block plans, the block level proposals for district level schemes are integrated together at the district level. These district plans are brought in at the state level with district level proposals for state level schemes in the districts and made into an integrated state plan. And such state plans we used to bring that to the Planning Commission and also when Mr. Hegde was its Deputy Chairman.

Going back to the block plan, after this is formulated, at the implementation stage, by looking at the two-way table I just talked about, you will know who will implement what, whether its the PWD or panchayats, and you give that power of implementation to the implementing authority. And the monitoring then is collective, through the committees, every quarter. And at the state level the same happens and so on.

I would mention that there was one shortcoming in our situation. Along with the class character representation, the Scheduled Caste/Scheduled Tribe representation has been more than proportionate. Total percentage is 28 per cent in the state; it is more than 30 per cent among the panchayat members. But womens' participation in panchayats varies between 12 and 15 per cent and we are not happy. I do not know what happened here, but we have decided to ensure that in our next panchayat elections there is one-third reservation for women.[1]

It is not simply a matter of bringing women into panchayats. If we are true to what we are saying, we have to combine it with the programme of joint *pattas* which include women members of the household as regards ownership. In other words, it is not simply redistributing but also ensuring land, joint ownership of both husband and wife in households that acquire land. It is very important to give women dignity. More than anything else in our country, it is the right of ownership of land to women that will ensure that husbands would not dare to desert them.

National Scenario

Back in 1987, we had introduced a highly decentralised incentive scheme for small savings collection. You know about the small savings schemes in every state where people keep their money in post offices and so forth and 75 per cent of that collection the state gets back as a loan. It is a very important source of revenue for the state. Under our decentralised incentive scheme, for each district we had set targets for small savings with this directive that if the district can cross that target, then 50 per cent of the extra amount the district will be able to retain for its development schemes. That immediately brought in results. Our small savings collection which was around Rs. 325 crores in 1987-88 increased to Rs. 1,000 crores in 1990-91.

But then, there was suddenly a change in the ground rules at the national level. The rate of interest on small savings is fixed by the Government of India, which also fixes the rate of return on mutual funds. Suddenly, the rate of return on mutual funds was made more attractive than that on small savings schemes. You know what happened – there was a massive shift of resource for all states from the small savings schemes, from which states benefit, to the mutual funds scheme, which is exclusively under the central financial institutions. And there was a loss of revenue by 40 per cent. West Bengal lost, I recall, Rs. 414 crores in a year.

Where did this money go? I place it before the JPC. There are reasons to apprehended that a very significant part of it could have found its way, through the mutual funds scheme, to the share market. Who gained? The JPC is enquiring into it. But who lost, we know: the small investors and the states. In a state where there is decentralised planning and people in the districts and the blocks had expectations of schemes being implemented out of that money, suddenly they did not find the money. Now, when you have introduced decentralisation and, therefore, there is direct accountability to people, it is all the more important that there should be a corresponding flow of funds, and at least not a disruption in the flow of funds, from the centre to the states. In the absence of decentralisation this remains a state level problem. But with decentralisation it becomes a problem at the ground level. And I would, therefore, strongly point out that we should not talk about decentralisation only at the level of states and below. It has to be at all levels: decentralisation from the centre to the states and to the districts.

Now, confronted with this crisis in our state, there is a third decision we are contemplating, that even the state level tax collection – the stamp duties, the motor vehicle tax, royalty on minor minerals and some others – should be devolved to the level of districts. By giving this power of major tax collection to districts we can involve the panchayats and people in stopping tax evasion. We could have an incentive in this scheme as well, that if a district crosses its tax collection target, half the extra amount it contributes it can retain for construction and maintenance of roads, school buildings, irrigation projects, etc. This would be the district's untied fund which it could use as it likes. And I have confidence that through such a scheme the tax collection will improve very significantly.

Decentralisation is not simply decentralisation of expenditure, it can include decentralisation of resource mobilisation as well. And the reason we want to do it, is the last point I want to make. You see, the block is not the terminus. Because a block, on an average, in any part of India is a collection of hundred villages. The block is still a distant point. From the block you have to go down not only to the *anchal* but to the village and not only to a mukhia or a panchayat representative but to people. We have started doing this in some districts. With respect to every scheme, beneficiary committees will have to be associated, they will have to be directly connected. And these committees will also be associated with resource mobilisation. In other words, we are taking the entire power of expenditure and resource mobilisation down to the level of the village, to the grassroots level.

These days, we find that in the name of liberalisation actually what is taking place is a centralisation of resources and decision-making power, from the States to the Centre. Mr. Sathe,[2] it has worsened since your time. And at the Centre you go to a ministry and it directs you to the finance ministry. In other words, within the central government there is a further centralisation towards the finance ministry and when you talk to the concerned person in the finance ministry, he will direct you to the IMF and the World Bank.

In other words, there is a concentration of power away from people, through the States to the Centre and through the Centre to Washington D.C! We want to do the opposite. We, in West Bengal, want to give back powers to the people. So this is our proposed alternative at the national level. And I think, in view of the serious problems being encountered in international socialist reconstruction, our experiment in democratic decentralisation may be of some relevance even in the international context. Thank you.

NOTES

1. The West Bengal panchayat elections held on May 30, 1993, implemented this provision.
2. A pointed reference to Mr. Vasant Sathe, former Cabinet Minister, sitting in the audience.

5

George Fernandes

DECENTRALISATION MULTIPRONGED APPROACH

SINCE we are discussing panchayati raj and decentralisation, it will be in the fitness of things if at least we try to conduct our discussion in *lok bhasha* (people's language), instead of English. I know that some people may have some difficulty in understanding me, but I hope you will bear with me.

We are here to commemorate the memory of Prof. Lakdawala. My friendship with him goes back thirty years. In 1963 our trade unions in Bombay launched a struggle against the faulty cost of living index. I was then imprisoned in Nagpur jail. Madhu Limaye was the leader of that struggle. We managed to bring life in Bombay to a standstill for ten whole days. Consequent upon that strike, the then Chief Minister of Maharashtra constituted a committee headed by Prof. Lakdawala to give its expert opinion on the cost of living index prepared by us on behalf of the Hind Mazdoor Panchayat. He submitted his report within three or four months. It was because of this report that millions of wage and salary earners, from a peon to a secretary to the government, not only of Bombay but of the whole country, benefitted. The distortions in the weightage given to various

---

Translated from Hindi

items in calculating the cost of living index were corrected. It is difficult to assess by how many additional thousand crore rupees, innumerable workers from all over the country, including people working in government offices and other establishments, have secured from Lakdawala's recommendations. It is true that the workers of Bombay fought against the unjust cost of living index but the credit for setting things right must go to Prof. Lakdawala.

My friendship with Prof. Lakdawala developed not merely in the context of the trade union movement. A time came in 1977 when we both became part of the government in Delhi. I was the Minister for Industries and Prof. Lakdawala became the Deputy Chairman of the Planning Commission. I used to consult him, discuss with him and seek his opinion on many matters pertaining to my ministry. His contribution to the New Industrial Policy of the Janata Government was enormous. Decentralisation was the main thrust of that policy. The District Industries Centres (DICs) became the basic units for taking industries to the people. It was under that policy that all the powers of the central and state governments were transferred to the DICs, working at the district level. Even today, those DICs are functioning. They have become weak, but they still survive. Prof. Lakdawala made his own significant contribution in giving concrete shape to this institution, which was an effort to concretize the idea of decentralisation.

He was the chairman of the Institute of Social Sciences as well. His concern for decentralisation found expression in the studies the Institute undertook, as the Director has pointed out a little while earlier.

After leaving the Planning Commission he became the chairman of the Centre for Monitoring Indian Economy (CMIE). During that period whenever I went to Bombay, with a few rare exceptions, I invariably dropped in at the CMIE office in Worli and spent an hour or two with him.

I want to remember him and pay my tributes to him not only as a friend but also as a votary of an alternative economic and political system in this country.

Decentralisation: Economic, Political and Financial

Shri Pranab Mukherjee, at the end of his inaugural speech, asked a question: Has the time come for decentralisation or not? When he posed this question I got a little rattled. There were two reasons. First, that if in Mahatma Gandhi's land and that too after 45 years of Independence, we are asking this question, then certainly something has basically gone wrong. Here I will talk not only of the Mahatma's views. Dr. Rammanohar Lohia was perhaps the greatest propagator of Gandhi's ideas. He also propounded the concept of a four-pillar state. He put this idea not only before the Socialist movement but the entire nation. In my view that was the most clear and concrete concept of decentralisation. It was not merely confined to economic decentralisation but encompassed the domain of political power. His own party, the Socialist party – for a while it was the PSP and then the S.S.P. – could not become strong enough to implement the idea of the four-pillar state for development and for restructuring and reconstructing Indian polity and society. All of us who call ourselves followers of Lohia, and there are a large number of such people, also have failed in this task. It is not a happy thought that 45 years after Independence, we have only reached a point where we are beginning to seriously pose this question of decentralisation.

There is another and more disturbing point. Prof. Ashim Dasgupta has aptly said at the conclusion of his speech that on the one hand, we organise seminars, hold discussions, write articles and even make laws in Parliament on decentralisation, panchayati raj and on how to transfer powers to the ordinary people. On the other hand, we have created a situation where important decisions affecting India's economic and political autonomy are taken outside the country, in Washington. In this situation, any discussion on decentralisation becomes futile, meaningless. And we seem to accept living in this hypocritical situation.

I think, that unless we grasp this basic fact that without decentralisation of our economic and political structure we cannot remove our poverty and backwardness, that we cannot achieve the goal of prosperity and social justice, we shall not be able to do anything. And more importantly, for those of us who accept this proposition, there is no option except to oppose and fight against the so-called New Economic Policy. Not opposing the New Economic Policy while at the same time talking of decentralisation means becoming a victim of an irreconcilable contradiction. I cannot see it in any other light. The IMF, the World Bank and other foreign powers are dictating to us the path of development we ought to follow. We are losing our freedom to determine our own future.

But there is yet another aspect. I wonder whether we, who talk of decentralisation, really believe in it? It appears that we talk of decentralisation but, somehow or the other, knowingly or unknowingly, we are inclined towards centralisation. Prof. Dasgupta briefly mentioned the working of the banking system, the Securities Exchange Bureau of India (SEBI) and postal savings. The question is not so much about postal savings because the money out of postal savings in a given state goes to that state for spending. The real problem is that of the credit-deposit ratio of the banking system within states. Here the reality is that there is an outflow of money from the poor states to metropolitan centres like Delhi and Bombay. These cities have a magnetic quality, they attract funds from the banks in poorer areas. They are flourishing at the cost of the poorer states. I do not have the latest data on the credit-deposit ratio of banks in West Bengal. Last year's data available clearly shows that West Bengal could reach the level of 55 per cent and that also after three to four years of serious efforts. For Bihar, which is the poorest state of the country, the credit-deposit ratio is just 39 percent; for Uttar Pradesh it is 40 percent. The poorer the state, the higher are the chances of outflow of money from the banking system of that state. This is another form of centralisation. If you go to the district level, and further, to the village level, you will find that the situation is deplorable. Most of the deposits made in the village branches of a bank go outside the village and the same condition is to be found in a poor district. Rarely is even a small fraction of the money deposited in the village branch of a bank spent for the development of that village. This is the situation all over the country.

Holistic Development Model

The question, therefore, is not merely one of establishing a particular system in the country, but of the whole approach to development. You can see it in our attitude to big and small projects. The same dichotomy prevails there. Take big projects like Narmada and Tehri. You bring money from foreign countries for constructing these big dams. Many people are displaced, they lose their land, their forest and all sources of their livelihood. They get completely ruined. So while on one hand, we construct big dams, choose the path of development based on large scale industrialization, in the same breath, we talk of decentralisation. Again, the contradictions involved in such an approach are ignored. A new thinking is needed, a holistic approach is necessary to build a new India, a better India, a just India.

The more I think on this, the more worried I become, because I am witness to how we all have become slaves of a particular civilisation. I am happy that today, here, we have been served plain water. Nowadays in ministerial and official meetings, mineral water, Bisleri, is served. Even if you go to the residence of political leaders you are not served plain water. Mr. Chairman, in your remarks, you referred to the gap which exists between ordinary people and the leadership. This gap has become enormously wide due to the kind of planning we have pursued during the last 45 years. The end result of this is that the policy-makers themselves have become aware that water supplied to ordinary people is not potable. And that is why the planners and the executors of those plans, the politicians, and administrators keep mineral water, Bisleri, costing ten to twelve rupees – I do not know the exact price – a bottle, in their homes. They know that water supplied through the local bodies is not pure.

We have been raising this problem of supply of pure drinking water in the villages for four decades and more. We have been saying that two to three lakh villages do not get quality drinking water. But now, those who control our destiny, by their behaviour, have demonstrated that pure drinking water is not available even in big cities. When I ordered Coca-Cola company to go out of India, I had a personal experience in my mind. When I was elected to Parliament in 1977, I was in prison. As soon as I came out of prison, I was made a minister in the union government. After a month or two I went on a tour of my constituency. The district magistrate was with me. At a small village I asked for water to drink. The district magistrate tried to prevent me from drinking the water which some villager brought, and said that it was not of potable quality. He had brought a crate of Coca-Cola and another crate of ice in the boot of his car for me. I could not accept such a situation. A few months later, I became the Minister for Industries and got the opportunity to throw out Coca-Cola from the country. I told them, our immediate task is to make drinking water available in the villages, so you please go. Once we have achieved this task, we will see about your drink. But see where we have reached. We now have the Bisleri culture. Without even a modicum of protest we have accepted that the tap water we get is not potable, that it is in fact dangerous to drink the water we get from our taps.

If there is a sharp variation between our goals and the present development model and the culture it has generated, we cannot ignore it. If we do not understand this contradiction, I am of the view that nothing substantial will result from whatever we may resolve. The first point which I want to make most forcefully is that there is a need for a complete change in our thinking. It is sad that our country is not fully prepared for it. In my view, the IMF-dictated policies and decentralisation are incompatible. Mr. Chairman, we are in agreement that decentralised development is not possible without decentralisation of political power. I am happy that Ashim Dasgupta has presented to us the experience of West Bengal in this respect, in such a beautiful manner. I would suggest that he does not stop at inviting some persons to Bengal to study their experience. I would request that he send some persons from his state to other states, to share Bengal's experiences with other parts of the country. This exercise will benefit the country immensely. It will be a great lesson if we understand that political and economic decentralisation are but two sides of the same coin, two wheels of the same cart. In the absence of either wheel, the cart cannot move.

This matter is not confined only to the development model. It is related to social strife and conflict as well. The proposed constitutional amendment stipulates 33 per cent reservation for women in all the three tiers of the panchayat system. The Hegde government in Karnataka enacted a similar provision years ago by reserving 25 percent seats for women, making it the first time anywhere in the world that such a large proportion of seats were reserved for women in elected bodies. When we were in government in Karnataka, we demonstrated how Karnataka politics could be fundamentally transformed through decentralisation.

Decentralisation of Administrative Structure

In the decentralised political structure we should try to change the existing administrative structure of the state. Let us talk of the bureaucracy first. The bureaucracy is using the country like a pasture for its benefit. It has no longer any relationship with the people. Of course, there are exceptions in everything, but we are not talking of exceptions but of the whole system. I have not come to this opinion today, this has been my view for years. Whenever we complained to Morarji Bhai that this bureaucracy was not allowing us to do anything, he would reply with a smile that the bureaucracy was like a horse whose movement depended on the quality of the horserider. But now I am of the opinion that the simile was not appropriate. We cannot even dream of decentralisation, political or economic, through a bureaucracy which is self perpetuating, which considers the entire country its pasture. Not only is this bureaucratic system an unfit instrument, it is also the greatest obstacle in the path of decentralisation.

Let me give an example of the police. In 1977 there used to be one Inspector General (IG) of Police for one whole state. Today we have six director-generals of police and now it is difficult to keep count of IGs in a state. Every year new posts of IGs are created in every state with a consequent increase in the number of IPS officers. You have talked about Delhi. It has been proposed that there should be three metropolitan councils for Delhi. Mr. Chairman, this proposal has not come out of any concept of decentralisation. If there are three metropolitan councils in Delhi, three IAS officers will be appointed as three municipal commissioners, three IAS officers will be appointed as deputy/additional commissioners. We will have three posts of IAS officers where today we have one. And this three-fold expansion is for those who have no achievements to their credit, either in the development of the country or a city. We can only experience their negative contributions in every field.

We think that America is a big, centralised country. In my opinion, though America is supposed to be a centralised state, it is one of the most decentralised countries in the contemporary world. The power of America is the power of the American people, not only of the American capitalists. Americans in a village elect their police officers. The law and order officials are elected and after that they are paid salaries. I am not suggesting that the best system will be to have every village select its own police. But I definitely would like a village panchayat to appoint its own police for the security of that village. There is no need for police recruited in Haryana to look after law and order in Maharashtra or for some Keralite to go to Bengal to look after law and order there. As far as law and order in a village is concerned, half-a-dozen director-generals or an even more enhanced number of senior officers cannot be of any help.

I have talked about women. Exceptions apart, there is hardly a village in our country where women are not ill-treated. But I have no hesitation in saying that the police, who are responsible for law and order, are the worst violaters of the dignity of women. Today we have heard the shocking news from Bengal that a village woman was raped by three police officers in a police station. The policemen who committed the heinous crime may have been from Bengal but certainly not from the same village or locality to which that hapless woman belonged. If you recruit a policeman and make him in charge of the security of the village he belongs to, no one will dare to kidnap a girl from that village and take her to the police station to rape her. What I am saying may appear to be a minor matter, but if we want to evolve a just system for the country, then, only by paying great attention to such minor matters, can we take steps to transfrom the entire prevailing system. I again want to emphasize that we should think about political, economic and administrative decentralisation together.

Decentralised Banking System

Dr. Dasgupta, you have talked about the bank scam. You have posed a specific question about the functioning of the Joint Parliamentary Committee. I believe that the system of control prevailing today is revealing its weakness because of its centralised character. We are in the process of unravelling many aspects of the scam. Many agencies, including the Joint Parliamentary Committee (JPC), are probing the matter. One common factor has emerged. The chairman or the managing director or the highest officer of every bank now says that he did not know anything, and everything happened in the back-room. Look, in this respect also, where has centralisation landed us? I do not accept their excuses. I am firmly of the opinion that they are fully aware that the back-room is not responsible. But they are using the back-room as a cover, though they will not succeed in their efforts. How capital meant for national development was made available by the centralised system to a few persons for speculation, has been a very disillusioning experience for the nation and has done incalculable harm to the whole country.

The more disturbing fact is that if an amount of thousand and five hundred crore rupees cannot be found in our account books, where did it disappear? What makes it worse is that the finance minister of the country asks rhetorically: "How big is this amount of three thousand crore rupees? Why so much noise about it?" People like us cannot help but be worried because, whatever the amount involved, such financial havoc has necessarily stemmed from a highly centralised banking system.

We firmly believe that whatever is possible to achieve through decentralisation, is not possible through centralization. There is no need for me to speak on corruption, because, you, Mr. Hegde, and others have spoken on it at length. I, however, firmly believe that wherever there is a mega project, there will be a mega scandal. Mr. Hegde has narrated about a Gram Sabha meeting which resolved the issue of the misappropriation of 60,000 rupees by the head of the Mandal Panchayat. It was raised at the beginning of the meeting and was resolved by the end of the meeting. The question of going to the JPC did not arise. So, even if we intend to find a solution to important moral questions thrown up by the situation, the system of decentralisation alone is the suitable solution. The discussion we have had in memory of Prof. Lakdawala, and which will continue in other fora, I am sure, will be helpful in resolving and deciding about all these issues.

INDEX